PERFECT

ASSERTIVENESS

Terry O'Brien is a best-selling author, columnist, consultant and motivational trainer. He is highly sought-after in the corporate as well as academic world, and has been training managers and providing counselling and consultancy over the past couple of decades. Author of hugely popular books on motivation, effective change and all that is 'un-Google-able', his writings focus on skill development and communication techniques. Terry O'Brien is a firm believer that 'infotainment' is a must for content to be effective, and his books are all about the three 'R's: Read, Record and Recall.

OTHER TITLES IN THE SERIES

Perfect Appraisal

Perfect Communication

Perfect CV

Perfect Interview

Perfect Leader

Perfect Management Skills

Perfect Marketing

Perfect Meeting

Perfect Negotiation

Perfect People Skills

Perfect Personality

Perfect Presentation

Perfect Salesmanship

Perfect Strategy

Perfect Time Management

PERFECT
ASSERTIVENESS

Get it right every time

Terry O'Brien

RUPA

Published by
Rupa Publications India Pvt. Ltd 2017
7/16, Ansari Road, Daryaganj
New Delhi 110002

Sales centres:
Allahabad Bengaluru Chennai
Hyderabad Jaipur Kathmandu
Kolkata Mumbai

The views and opinions expressed in this book are the author's
own and the facts are as reported by him/her which have been
verified to the extent possible, and the publishers
are not in any way liable for the same.

ISBN: 978-81-291-4542-0

First impression 2017

10 9 8 7 6 5 4 3 2 1

Typeset by Chetan Sharma

Contents

Introduction   *vii*

1. Assertiveness training   1

2. Responses: Passive, aggressive and assertive   5

3. Parameters of assertive behaviour   11

4. Negativity in being passive   13

5. Range of negative-aggressive behaviour   19

6. Assertiveness for self-confidence and   22
    self-esteem

7. Communicating assertively   25

8. 'I' factor   30

9. Passive behaviour   35

10. Assertiveness skills   39

11. Where to begin?   44

12. Benefits of being assertive   46

13. Modes of communication   49

14. Being assertive   55

15. Draw the fine line   63

Introduction

This book will help you to:

- understand 'I', 'me' and 'myself'.

- understand more about assertiveness and its importance as a life skill.

- understand more about yourself and about why you behave in certain ways.

- recognise the possibilities of changing and liberating the potential to be 'yourself'.

- use realistic tips for putting assertiveness into practice.

Man management is the essence of success and it begins from us. In order to get the most from life, whatever our role, we have to work at sorting out our relationships with other people. The skill of assertiveness helps us to do that. One has to hone one's skills to become more effective in relating to others in personal life and at work. However, the first relationship which we should address, and often the one we neglect, is with ourselves. Even though this book makes little claim to originality or depth, it tells you exactly how to spend some time constructively working on your relationship with yourself. In the exercise of assertiveness, it is useful to have a toolkit to carry around which can help one deal with what comes along. Indeed, assertiveness is a major tool.

There are five levels of self-discovery—behaviour, feelings, vision, values and self-image.

Behaviour: What we do, tells us much about who we are.

Feelings: Feelings tell us even more than behaviour.

Vision: Our thoughts and beliefs determine our feelings.

Values: Our values influence our thoughts and beliefs.

Self-image: This is the core—the most tender yet the powerful part of 'me'—the 'real me'.

So let us, now, take hold of not only the situations but ourselves! This book is based on the premise of experience and learning.

Indeed, here is all you need to get it right every time!

Assertiveness Training

EMPHASIS OF ASSERTIVENESS TRAINING

- An assertive person is one who acts in a way he or she respects. The emphasis is on being respected (self-respect and others' respect), rather than being liked.

- The emphasis is on not letting ourselves be pressurised or manipulated.

- The emphasis is on adequate behaviour. Inadequate behaviour leads to self-doubt. Adequate behaviour breaks this vicious circle.

- The emphasis is on not letting other people define your role for you to the point where you stop being yourself.

- The emphasis is on appropriate behaviour.

- The emphasis is on doing what you really want to do, not necessarily what you like to do.

- Assertiveness is not aggressiveness. Aggressiveness provokes counter-aggression. Assertiveness does not.

- The emphasis is on developing the ability to expand your social network, if you wish, and choosing appropriate levels of communication.

- The thrust is towards not acting out of fear and to live up to your own expectations and goals.

ASSERTIVENESS TRAINING

Improving your knowledge and your ability to communicate assertively can help you to be more successful. Assertiveness is not a one-size-fits-all approach to relate to others. It helps you to respect your own and other people's needs, wants and rights.

Assertiveness is important in all forms of communication, for instance, when you give or receive compliments, make or respond to requests, or handle difficult circumstances or relationships. Relating assertively does not guarantee that the other person will be equally assertive. As a style of communication, assertiveness is healthier for you and others, and more likely to lead you to success than either aggressive or passive behaviour.

Practising Assertiveness

Discuss the main differences between aggressive, submissive and assertive behaviour. Get into groups of three (If you want to form groups of four, appoint two observers and switch roles so that each participant gets to play all parts). The instructor shall lead the groups through each play, one at a time.

After discussing the given situations, answer these questions.

- What did you feel about the conversation?
- Was the interaction assertive? If not, why?

Situation one: Teammate B puts extra effort to create a great-looking graph for the report.

Person A: Sincerely compliments B

Person B: Responds assertively

Person C: Observes

Situation two: Your team has gone out to celebrate the successful completion of the Literature Review. While eating, you notice that teammate C has a piece of broccoli stuck between his/her teeth, which he/she seems unaware of.

Person A: Observes

Person B: Responds assertively

Person C: Assertively handles the interaction with B

Situation three: It is normally your job to send an email to all your team members after class, summarising team decisions and reminding the team of agreed-upon tasks. Today, however, you are scheduled to retake an algebra exam right after class. Make an assertive request of teammate B to write and send this email to the team on your behalf.

Note: This is the second time you've made such a request.

Person A: Responds assertively

Person B: Observes

Person C: Analyses the overall reactions

Situation four: It is the fourth week of your team project and teammate B has been late to three sessions, missing crucial instructions and work time. Once again, he/she walks in thirty minutes late.

Person A: Handles the situation assertively

Person B: Responds assertively

Person C: Observes

Responses: Passive, Aggressive And Assertive

Passive	Aggressive	Assertive
Indifferent	Attacks verbally or physically	Speaks clearly and confidently
Lifeless	Hostile	Honest
Doesn't care	Sarcastic	Deals with anger
Avoids the problem	Blames others	Addresses the problem appropriately
Not confident	Selfish	Considers the rights of the other person
Callous	Opinionated	Cautious and mindful
Builds anger	Acts in anger	Active and composed
Hopes that needs will be met	Demanding	Cares about 'self'
Non-aggressive	Emotional	Balanced

PASSIVE BEHAVIOUR

Passive behaviour involves saying nothing in response. It is trying to keep your feelings to yourself; hiding them from others. It may also lead to the extreme of concealing your feelings from yourself. Passive behaviour is often dishonest and involves letting other people violate your right to be treated with respect and dignity.

AGGRESSIVE BEHAVIOUR

Aggressive behaviour involves expressing your feelings indirectly through hostile statements and actions, insults, sarcasm, labels and put-downs. Aggressive behaviour involves expressing thoughts, feelings and opinions in a way that violates others' rights to be treated with respect and dignity.

ASSERTIVE BEHAVIOUR

Assertive behaviour involves describing your feelings, thoughts, opinions and preferences directly to another person in an honest and appropriate way that is respectful for both. It enables you to act in your own best interests, to stand up for yourself without undue anxiety, to express honest feelings comfortably, and to exercise personal rights without denying the rights of others. Assertive behaviour is direct, honest, self-enhancing, not hurtful to others and is appropriate for the receiver and the situation.

Many people feel that if they assert themselves, others will think of their behaviour as aggressive. There is a huge difference between being assertive and being aggressive.

Assertive people state their opinions while being respectful of others. Aggressive people attack or ignore others' opinions in favour of their own. Passive people don't state their opinions at all.

Differences between passive, aggressive and assertive behaviour

Passive Person	Aggressive Person	Assertive Person
Is afraid to speak up	Interrupts and 'talks over' others	Speaks openly
Speaks softly	Speaks loudly	Uses a conversational tone
Avoids looking at people	Glares and stares at others	Makes good eye contact
Shows little or no expression	Intimidates by using expressions	Shows expression that match the message being conveyed
Slouches and withdraws	Stands rigidly, crosses arms and invades the personal space of others	Relaxes and adopts an open stance and expression
Isolates self from groups	Controls groups	Participates in groups

Passive Person	Aggressive Person	Assertive Person
Agrees with others despite a difference of opinion	Considers only own feelings and/or makes demands of others	Keeps to the point
Values 'self' less than others	Values 'self' more than others	Values 'self' equal to others
Hurts self to avoid hurting others	Hurts others to avoid being hurt	Tries to hurt no one (including self)
Does not reach goals and may not even have one	Reaches goals but hurts others in the process	Usually reaches goals without hurting others
'You're okay; I'm not.'	'I'm okay; you're not.'	'I'm okay; you're okay.'

Characteristics And Examples Of Passive Behaviour

- Belittling yourself or your achievements
- Not saying 'No' (when you should)
- Not saying 'Yes' (when you want to)
- Over-apologising
- Letting others run your life
- Never sharing your ideas
- Putting up with threatening or manipulative behaviours
- Withdrawal

Characteristics And Examples Of Aggressive Behaviour

- Threats and intimidation
- Sarcasm
- Manipulation
- Name calling, belittling or insulting
- Demanding
- Blaming
- Hostility
- Violence

Characteristics And Examples Of Passive-Aggressive Behaviour (Combining The Worst Of Both)

- Hidden hostility
- Agreeing to do something but not doing it
- Sabotaging someone behind the scene
- Gossip and back biting

Characteristics And Examples Of Assertive Behaviour

- Accepting compliments comfortably
- Using 'I need...', 'I want...' and 'I feel...' statements to express your needs, wants, feelings or concerns
- Taking all parties' interests into account
- Being comfortable saying both 'Yes' or 'No', as appropriate
- Being courteous
- Being honest and concise in expressing feelings
- Speaking clearly and maintaining eye contact

Positive-assertive behaviour is the 'ability to respond'; negative-assertive behaviour is the 'capacity to retreat'.

Parameters Of Positive-Assertive Behaviour

- *Managing Emotions:* Being open in expressing wishes, thoughts and feelings, and encouraging others to do likewise.

- *Active Listening:* Listening to the views of others and responding appropriately, whether in agreement with those views or not.

- *Delegation Skills:* Accepting responsibilities and being able to delegate to others.

- *Appreciation and Gratitude:* Regularly expressing appreciation of others for what they have done or are doing.

- *Self-Control:* Maintaining self-control.

- *Being Fair:* Behaving as an equal to others.

Parameters Of Assertive Behaviour

Assertiveness is a skill that you need. This is a skill regularly referred to in social and communication skills' training. Being assertive means being able to stand up for your own; it also means standing up for other people's rights in a collected, calm and positive way, without being either aggressive or passively accepting what is not right.

Assertiveness means standing up for your personal rights—expressing thoughts, feelings and beliefs in direct, honest and appropriate ways. However, while being assertive, we should always respect the thoughts, feelings and beliefs of other people. Those who behave assertively always respect the thoughts, feelings and beliefs of other people as well as their own.

Assertiveness fortifies you to express feelings, wishes, wants and desires appropriately and is an important personal and interpersonal skill. It is a benchmark needed in all your interactions with people, whether at home or at work. It can help you to express yourself in a clear, open and reasonable way, without undermining your own or others' rights.

Assertiveness enables individuals to act in their own best interests, to stand up for themselves without undue anxiety, to express honest feelings comfortably and to express personal rights without denying the rights of others.

Negativity In
Being Passive

Responding in a passive or non-assertive way tends to mean compliance with the wishes of others and can undermine individual rights and self-confidence. The use of either passive or aggressive behaviour in interpersonal relationships can have undesirable consequences for those you are communicating with and it may well hinder positive moves forward.

- *Fear of not being liked*—Many people adopt a passive response because they have a strong need to be liked by others. Such people do not regard themselves as equals because they place greater weight on the rights, wishes and feelings of others.

- *Failure to communicate*—Being passive results in a failure to communicate thoughts or feelings and people doing things they really do not want to do, in the hope that they might please others. They allow others to take responsibility, to lead and make decisions for them.

- *Say 'Yes'*—A classic passive response is offered by those who say 'Yes' to requests when they actually want to say 'No'.

- *Being less positive*—Being passive or non-assertive may mean compliance with the wishes of others and can undermine individual rights and self-confidence.

- *Taken for granted*—If you become known as a person who cannot say 'No', you will be loaded with tasks by one and all; a trash can for all!

- *Not to be unpleasant*—Being more assertive does not involve being unpleasant to people and getting away with behaviour which upsets a team or having a dictatorial management style.

- *Mutual respect*—Being assertive is about respecting yourself enough to state what you want from other people. It is also about respecting other people and their right to express their needs.

Signs That You Are Being Passive-Aggressive

- Unable to express emotions
- Perpetual negativity
- Aggressive behaviour
- Putting the blame on others
- Being misunderstood
- Being unreasonable
- Always exaggerating
- Negative even in the best of times

ASSESS YOUR PASSIVITY

Assess your personal interaction style. It's important for you to understand your personal style before you decide to change it. If you are already being assertive in most areas of your life, you may only need to make minor adjustments. There is a fine line between being assertive and being aggressive.

Not Voicing Your Opinion

- Remaining quiet most of the time
- Saying 'Yes' when you really want to say 'No'
- Taking on more responsibility even when your plate is already full

Explore The Fear

- When you find yourself not standing up for yourself or struggling to say 'No' to others
- You're afraid to displease other people

What I Fear Will Happen If I Am More Assertive

What evidence do I have that the person will not retaliate? What I think will actually happen? What can I do to protect myself from the retaliation?

Sometimes you may refrain from being assertive because you don't want to hurt the other person's feelings. However, sometimes people will misinterpret your intentions even if your assertion is justified. You should not do what you don't want to do or refrain from sticking up for yourself because you're afraid of hurting someone else.

Release The Guilt

Harbouring guilt, when there's no basis for it, is neither fair to you nor is it healthy for your self-esteem.

Learn From Your Passivity

When you do what you don't want to do, it usually doesn't feel pleasant. Similarly, it feels awful when you find yourself being someone's doormat. So take some time to reflect on how it makes you feel when you are overly passive. Remind yourself that you do not have to feel bad about yourself. Learn to become more assertive.

Saying 'No'

Decide what you want to do and don't want to do. If you're a little more passive than you'd like to be, chances are that you often find yourself saying 'Yes' when you really want to say 'No'. This can create internal stress and a lot of resentment towards the other person. To avoid this, it's important to first figure out what you want to do and what you don't. When someone asks you to do something, ask yourself if it's really something that you want to do. If you find yourself saying that it won't be so bad, stop and ask yourself again if it's something that you really want to do. If you want to do it, then you won't have to convince yourself.

Say that you will not be able to do an assignment today.

At first, this may seem a little awkward because you're used to always saying 'Yes'. However, it's important to set boundaries with others.

Being assertive has many benefits.

- Greater self-confidence
- More respect from others
- Better self-esteem
- Improved decision-making
- Increased job satisfaction
- Better relationships

Repeat The Statement In A Word Or Two

If others are used to your compliance, they may show some resistance when you start saying 'No'. However, it is important for you to remain firm. Keep shortening your 'no' statement by a word or two, each time the person tries to insist. If the person continues to insist, it's time to be very direct by simply saying 'No'.

Discuss Alternatives

At times it may be difficult to say 'No'. For example, if keeping your job is a priority, you probably shouldn't just tell your supervisor 'No' and walk away. When you are in a bind and just saying 'No' isn't an option, then try offering alternatives instead. For example, you could say: 'Can I suggest another idea?'

Exit The Conversation

You may continue to get pushed even though you have made it clear that you are unable to comply with the request. At this point, it's probably time to end the conversation so that the situation doesn't escalate.

Practising Being Assertive

Make the decision to be more assertive. You must commit to make the change in order to start seeing results. Thinking about why you want to be more assertive would be helpful.

Some consequences of being overly passive

- Frustration with yourself may occur as you keep asking yourself how you managed to let that happen.

- Resentment can occur because you may begin to feel that you're being taken advantage of.

- Violence and verbal aggression can occur when frustration builds up and you respond inappropriately and lose control.

- Depression can result due to a sense of helplessness and feeling that you have no control over the situation.

5

Range Of Negative-Aggressive Behaviour

- Rushing someone unnecessarily
- Telling rather than asking
- Ignoring someone
- Not considering others' feelings
- Not empathising

There is a two-way conduit: response and approach.

It can be a frightening or distressing experience to be spoken to aggressively and the receiver can be left wondering what instigated such behaviour or what he or she has done to deserve the aggression.

Different people behave assertively in different ways. It is not a skill for cloning. We are all so different. Our uniqueness is a treasure to be celebrated. We don't have to be assertive in the same way as somebody else. But we can be aware of our own self, informed about the concept of assertiveness and determined to live our life in a way that allows us to achieve our goals. Being yourself is a key to contentment and the more you understand yourself, your behaviour and the behaviour of others, the more opportunity it gives you to be your best.

Assertiveness can be interpreted through:

- behaviour,
- self-confidence and self-esteem,
- communication, and
- being able to fulfil our needs.

When we behave assertively, we are in control of ourselves, and are not controlling others. Controlling one person is enough; no wonder we get exhausted trying to manipulate other people.

Imagine a situation: A person comes to a meeting—papers hugged to the chest, head down and mumbling a greeting. Do you think this person is going to have something interesting to say, or do you dismiss him/her in a split second?

On the other hand, somebody who enters the room full of their own self-importance, hustling people to make a start and obviously determined to put their own needs first is likely to turn people off for different reasons.

The person who walks in looking organised, making eye contact with a friendly smile and a greeting is going to have a far more favourable effect. We are likely to be warm to them, not feel threatened and actually look forward to hearing what they have to say. This is the person who is most likely to achieve his or her aims assertively.

KNOW THE 'YOU'

Which one of these approaches is nearest to describing you? Write 'Yes', 'No' or 'Sometimes' to answer the following.

- Do you make comfortable eye contact with people when you greet them?
- If you join a group of people, do you scan all of its members?
- In general, do you stand with your head up, shoulders back and feet apart?
- Do you speak clearly and directly, keeping your voice calm and controlled?
- Do you show interest in other people by smiling and responding to them?
- When do you appear confident and in control?
- When don't you appear confident and in control?
- What would help you to transfer that comfort and confidence from one situation to another?

Ask people to help you answer these questions. Maybe you haven't been able to answer with a straight 'Yes' or 'No', so think about specific situations.

Note: When we behave assertively, we give the impression of being comfortable with ourselves and of being happy to occupy the space we are in.

6

Assertiveness For Self-Confidence And Self-Esteem

Think about a situation where you have been in disagreement with somebody and you have failed to state your point of view. How do you feel afterwards? Angry? Let down? Do you replay the whole incident adding what you could, should or wish you had said and frequently chastise yourself for not saying those things? You may become more and more angry but really the anger is not with the other person, it is with yourself—for not standing your ground, for not being quick-witted, articulate or brave enough to counter the attack, however subtle, from the other person. 'Why did I let them speak to me like that?', 'Why didn't I just say it?' and 'Who do they think they are?' The more we chew over this, the more we eat into our self-esteem. We feel that we have let ourselves down, allowed someone to 'get the better of us'. The incident leaves an aftertaste of awful feeling. On the other hand, when we find ourselves in a potentially difficult situation with somebody, and we handle it well, we walk away feeling good about ourselves. It is usually the negative feelings which hang around.

When we are assertive, we feel good about ourselves because we let other people know how they can treat us. We don't feel intimidated by other people because we have a realistic, healthy measure of our own self-worth.

Being assertive means speaking up for yourself, being able to express your opinions and feelings. Assertiveness is important for a healthy self-esteem and for your overall well-being.

It can be very difficult to be assertive when you have low self-esteem. You may believe that you don't deserve to be heard or that your opinion doesn't matter. You may put other people's needs before your own, which means that your own needs are not met. Alternatively, you could be afraid of speaking up for yourself. You get anxious or worry about what others will say or do, or how you will cope with it. Not being assertive makes it easy for you to be ignored, taken advantage of or even bullied. Consequently, you may feel sad, depressed, frustrated or angry. It lowers your self-esteem.

YOU CAN BECOME MORE ASSERTIVE

Indeed, you can learn to become assertive. A good starting point is changing your beliefs about yourself. It is important to know that everyone, including you, is entitled to their opinion, to have feelings and to express them. You have the right to make your own choices and decisions. It is okay to say 'No' from time to time and to be yourself. Becoming more assertive is a skill that requires practice and persistence. However, it is well worth the effort.

Self-esteem is about how we value ourselves, our beliefs and perceptions about who we are and what we are capable of. Our self-esteem can be misaligned with other people's perception of who we are. Interestingly, self-esteem has little to do with actual talent or ability. It's quite possible for someone who is good at something to have poor self-esteem, while someone who struggles at a particular topic might have good self-esteem.

It is easy to see how lack of self-esteem can influence how a person behaves, not to mention what they achieve in their lives.

7

Communicating Assertively

When we communicate assertively, we say what we mean and mean what we say by giving clear, straight-forward messages.

BE DIRECT

If there is something to be said, then don't soft-pedal around, go on and say it. Avoid the tendency to use preambles like: 'I know you're really busy but...', 'I'm ever so sorry to trouble you...', 'You'll probably think I'm awful saying this...'

These give the other person an opportunity to anticipate what we might be about to say and adopt a defensive or dismissive attitude. It is far more effective to directly state what we are trying to put across to somebody. That doesn't mean that we have to be rude, abrupt or unpleasant. It merely means that we give the impression of having considered what we want to communicate before we actually launch into sound. This gains us respect from others and prevents clouding of the message.

BE APPROPRIATE

Communication is most successful when the 'sender' is sensitive to the 'receiver'. We should change our style of communicating to suit the person we are with; a degree of sensitivity to the other person will help. For example, if you are in the company of an elderly relative, who is expressing views about the 'youth of today' or the 'downfall of society', it might be appropriate to go along with them rather than express rational arguments to prove them wrong! If you are making a point to your boss, then your style might be different from that of criticising your partner. Not only the person, but the time and place should also influence how appropriate it is to assert oneself. It might be more appropriate to let some things go.

TAKE RESPONSIBILITY

'I think...', 'In my opinion...' and 'My understanding is...' are all far more effective ways of putting across our view than 'You are...', 'That's not right...' and 'It isn't like that…'

We have the right to our opinions but ours is not the only opinion. People will be far more receptive to being told things about themselves if it is offered as your opinion rather than a universal statement.

Consider these statements.

- Your driving is terrible.
- That outfit doesn't suit you.
- You can't say that.
- You never clean the bath properly.

- You were horrible to me last night.
- That won't work; you should do it like this.

The responses are likely to be defensive or confrontational. Taking ownership of what you are saying will result in the other person being less threatened and more amenable to listening to you.

REMAIN CALM AND IN CONTROL

It is difficult to be assertive when your shoulders are hunched right up to your earlobes, your fists are clenched and your face is red. Taking deep breaths and letting some of the tension drain from you will help. Being assertive spontaneously is more difficult than when we've had time to prepare what we want to say. But a few seconds spent taking control of emotions will ensure that your brain is in gear before your tongue starts working. Of course, it's not only our words which communicate our message— our body language speaks volumes. By controlling the tone and volume of your voice, you can make the message less emotional. By ensuring that your body is relaxed and in tune with the words you are saying, you become more effective.

BE WILLING TO LISTEN

The most overlooked aspect of communication is listening. People often think that good communication skills are about being articulate, telling a good tale, having a wide vocabulary. Yes, all of these are important, but the ability and willingness to listen to others is more important. We tend to fall into the category of either listening distractedly—allowing other things, whether in our head or around us to interfere—or dismissively, filtering only the bits which we want to take in. When we are listening to somebody, we need to suspend judgement and emotion until we have heard them out and understood.

Mutual respect is a vital aspect of assertiveness. Listening to the other person's point of view is as important as expressing our own view of a situation. When we are listening to somebody as well as putting across our own views, we are actually more in control and, therefore, more assertive.

LISTENING SKILLS

While the other person is talking, do you often/sometimes/never:

- rehearse what you are going to say?
- wish they would get to the point quickly?
- interrupt?
- mind-read?
- judge them by appearance or accent?
- filter what you already think/want to think?
- daydream?

Most of us do some of these some of the time. We might think we are listening but we're not. When we communicate assertively, we respect the other person's right to put their views across. They can't do this if we are not listening to them. Don't just hear; try to listen!

ASSERTIVENESS FOR BEING YOURSELF

When we are assertive, we state what we think, what we feel and what we want. In order to do this, we have to put some thought into really understanding what it is that we think, feel and want. This can mean that you have to let some things go—after all, with every gain, there is loss. As you learn more about yourself and assertiveness, you will be able to weigh what your profit and loss will be in handling situations more assertively. Balance your books to achieve a huge net profit!

8

'I' Factor

Assertive communication involves the use of 'I' statements, such as 'I need some help…' Assertiveness is a way of making sure that your needs are met while still considering the needs of others.

Assertive communication is the straight-forward and open expression of your needs, desires, thoughts and feelings. Assertive communication involves advocating your own needs while still considering and respecting the needs of others.

If you suffer from Social Anxiety Disorder (SAD), communicating assertively may seem difficult at first.

Many people mistake assertiveness for aggressiveness, but assertiveness is actually the balanced middle ground between aggressiveness and passivity. Speaking assertively is respecting everyone's needs and rights—including your own—and it helps you to maintain boundaries in relationships.

If you adopt a passive communication style, it may enable you to avoid conflict but it will most certainly leave you feeling anxious, depressed and helpless; it will also cause frustration and discomfort to those around you. Learning to communicate assertively is not selfish, but rather an effective way of negotiating social encounters.

There are many misconceptions about what it means to be assertive. People who communicate assertively are not pushy. They do not disregard the feelings of others to get what they want, as is the case with aggressive communication. Instead, assertive communication involves expressing your feelings, needs and desires in a non-judgemental and non-threatening way. Assertive communication can be considered helpful as it enables you to give clear information about what you need to know. By doing so, in a non-threatening manner, you also give others the opportunity to refuse your requests if your needs conflict with their needs.

Assertive statements generally begin with the word 'I'. They directly express what you are thinking or feeling. Being assertive does not mean stepping on the toes of others or berating them. The goal of being assertive is to negotiate in a way that benefits everyone.

Here are some examples of assertive statements.

- I enjoyed talking with you.
- I like to watch romantic movies.
- I feel hurt that you talked about me behind my back.
- I know that the children come first, but I feel sad that we don't spend any time alone.

The next time you are feeling angry or resentful, consider how you are communicating it. If you suffer from SAD, you have probably developed a passive communication style. By learning to be more assertive, you will reduce anxiety and improve your relationships with others.

Assertive communication can strengthen your relationships, reducing stress from conflict. It will provide you with social support in difficult times. A polite but assertive 'No' to excessive requests from others will enable you to avoid overloading your schedule and promote balance in your life. Assertive communication can also help you handle difficult family members, friends and co-workers more easily, reducing drama and stress.

These assertive communication steps can help you develop a healthy communication style and relieve you of stress.

Be Factual, Not Judgemental

Be factual, not judgemental, about what you don't like. Here's an example.

Your friend, who habitually arrives late, has shown up twenty minutes late for a lunch date.

Inappropriate: You're so rude! You're always late.

Assertive communication: We were supposed to meet at 11.30 a.m. but now it's 11.50 p.m.

Be Accurate (Don't Judge Or Exaggerate)

Be accurate about the effects of this behaviour. Don't exaggerate, label or judge; just describe.

Inappropriate: Now, the lunch is ruined.

Assertive communication: Now, I have less time to spend at lunch because I still need to be back to work by 1 p.m.

'I' Messages

Simply put, if you start a sentence with 'You', it comes off as more of a judgement or an attack and puts people on the defensive, for instance, 'You need to stop that!'

If you start with 'I', the focus is more on how you are feeling and how you are affected by their behaviour, for instance, 'I'd like it if you'd stop that.'

Put It All Together

Here's a great formula that puts it all together.

'When you [something about them/their behaviour], I feel [your feelings].'

This statement is a responsible way of letting people know how their behaviour affects you. For example: When you yell, I feel attacked.

List Behaviour, Results And Feelings

A more advanced variation of this formula includes the results of their behaviour.

'When you [something about them/their behaviour], then [results of their behaviour], and I feel [your feelings].'

Here is an example.

When you arrive late, I have to wait and I feel frustrated.

While communicating:

- make sure your body reflects confidence. Stand up straight, look people in the eye and relax.
- use a firm, but pleasant tone.

- don't assume you know what the other person's motives are, especially if you think they're negative.

- (when in a discussion) don't forget to listen and ask questions! It's important to understand the other person's point of view as well.

- try to think win-win. See if you can find a compromise or a way for those involved.

9

Passive Behaviour

Passive behaviour is putting others' preferences before your own needs. Passive behaviour is also connected with submissive behaviour as both passive and submissive people tend to give others authority over themselves. Passive behaviour is to direct blame internally rather than towards external factors responsible for a given situation. Passive behaviour draws criticism and a passive person shies away from any kind of conflict, often leading to false acceptance of blame when another person goes on the offensive.

CHARACTERISTICS OF PASSIVE BEHAVIOUR

Hesitant, Approval-Seeking Speech

Passive individuals often seek the approval of others. They are incredibly fearful of upsetting others so they attempt to soften the impact of their comments through permission seeking. This often results in rambling statements which do not seem to say a whole. For example:

- Would you mind if I…

- I wouldn't normally say this but…

- I don't mean to be rude, but I was thinking that if it was okay with you…

Broken Speech Pattern

As they lack confidence, passive people tend to lack any form of certainty when they are expressing their opinions. You will hear them stop and hesitate. Their speech pattern will lack any rhythm or flow. The hesitations are often accompanied by 'e-r-r's and 'u-m-m's.

Belittling Their Own Views

The fear of upsetting others often results in them belittling their own views before they have even expressed them. Rather than wait for someone else to comment on their views, they try to soften the blow by striking first. For example:

- I'm no expert but...
- I have been known to be wrong but...

Putting The Preferences Of Others First

Passive behaviour leads individuals to place a higher value on the preferences and needs of others than they place on their own. They eagerly demonstrate that they are willing to sweep their own preferences aside. For example:

- I would like to...but if you would rather do something else...
- I don't want to be awkward but...

Overpowering Self-Criticism

We are all fallible, but passive people often struggle to accept that. While they may make few demands of others, they make very high, often unrealistic, demands of themselves.

When they fail to meet these, they often resort to extremely harsh self-criticism. If something goes wrong, they tend not to see the role played by others. Instead, they place the full blame on themselves. For example:

- I can't believe that I messed that up.
- I should have been able to get that right.

Self-Deprecating

While many people use self-deprecation as a form of humour, passive people tend to be quite serious when they resort to it. They put themselves down at the first opportunity, over the smallest things, often to the bewilderment of anyone within earshot. For example:

- Could I be any more pathetic?
- I am so stupid!

Soft-Spoken With Declining Volume

Passive people are usually very soft-spoken. They tend to lack confidence both in themselves and what they have to say. Therefore, keeping their voice down helps them to avoid drawing attention to themselves. As they approach the end of what they have to say, their volume lowers and tapers off.

Avoiding Eye Contact

Avoiding eye contact is one of the most common signs of passive behaviour. Due to lack of confidence, shame, guilt and a host of other negative emotions, passive people are unable to look into the eyes of the other person. They try to look away, often at the ground, in order to avoid eye contact.

Discomfort

Whether with their facial expressions or their body language, passive people send clear signals of discomfort. Even when they are trying to act confident, their appearance of discomfort will be a giveaway.

Passive behaviour is driven by the need for the approval of others. Rather than risk upsetting them, you put their preferences and needs before yours. This is not healthy behaviour. It is important to have respect for others, but you will never accomplish your goals and dreams unless you learn to give them the respect they merit. Passive behaviour is ineffective because there is only so much sacrifice you can make. Eventually, you will snap, either with yourself or with the people whom you have been trying to please. Neither of these outcomes is desirable as they can damage both your health and your relationships. The list above is certainly not exhaustive but it will provide you with a good idea of the behaviours which you need to be looking out for. If you find yourself displaying any of these behaviours, do not be harsh on yourself. Simply identify the changes you need to make and make them. It will take a little time but you will become a more assertive person.

10

Assertiveness Skills

Assertiveness is a skill regularly referred to in social and communication skills' training. Being assertive means being able to stand up for your own or other people's rights in a calm and positive way, without being either aggressive or passively accepting what is 'wrong'.

Assertive individuals are able to get their point across without upsetting others or becoming upset themselves.

Although everyone acts in passive and aggressive ways from time to time, such ways of responding often arise from a lack of self-confidence and are, therefore, inappropriate ways of interacting with others.

This chapter examines the rights and responsibilities of assertive behaviour. Indeed assertiveness can benefit you. It will help you build self-esteem.

Assertiveness means standing up for your personal rights—expressing thoughts, feelings and beliefs in direct, honest and appropriate ways.

It is important to note that those who behave assertively always respect the thoughts, feelings and beliefs of other people as well.

Assertiveness means being able to express feelings, wishes, wants and desires appropriately and it is an important personal and interpersonal skill. In all your interactions with other people, assertiveness can help you to express yourself in a clear, open and reasonable way, without undermining your own or others' rights.

Assertiveness enables individuals to act in their own best interests, to stand up for themselves without undue anxiety, to express honest feelings comfortably and to assert personal rights without denying the rights of others.

Passive, Aggressive And Assertive

Assertiveness is often seen as the balance point between passive and aggressive behaviours, but it's probably easier to think of them as three points of a triangle.

BEING ASSERTIVE

Being assertive involves taking into consideration your own and other people's rights, wishes, wants, needs and desires.

Assertiveness means encouraging others to be open and honest about their views, wishes and feelings, so that both parties act appropriately.

Assertive behaviour includes:

- being open in expressing wishes, thoughts and feelings and encouraging others to do likewise.

- listening to the views of others and responding appropriately, whether in agreement with those views or not.

- accepting responsibilities and being able to delegate to others.

- appreciating others for what they have done or are doing.

- being able to admit mistakes and apologise.

- maintaining self-control.

- behaving as an equal with others.

Those who struggle to behave assertively, may find that they behave either aggressively or passively. Being assertive is a core communication skill. Being assertive means that you express yourself effectively and stand up for your point of view, while also respecting the rights and beliefs of others. Being assertive can also help boost your self-esteem and earn others' respect.

Assertiveness is the quality of being self-assured and confident without being aggressive. In the field of psychology and psychotherapy, it is a learnable skill and mode of communication. In fact, assertiveness is singled out as a behavioural skill taught by many personal development experts. Assertiveness is often linked to self-esteem.

The goals of assertiveness training include:

- increased awareness of personal rights.

- differentiating between non-assertiveness and assertiveness.

- differentiating between passive–aggressiveness and aggressiveness.

- learning both verbal and non-verbal assertiveness skills.

As a communication style and strategy, assertiveness is thus distinguishable from both aggression and passivity. How people deal with personal boundaries, their own and those of other people, helps to distinguish between these three concepts. Passive communicators do not defend their own personal boundaries and thus allow aggressive people to abuse or manipulate them. Passive communicators are also typically not likely to risk trying to influence anyone. Aggressive people do not respect the personal boundaries of others and thus are likely to harm others while trying to influence them. A person communicates assertively by overcoming the fear of speaking his/her mind or trying to influence others, but doing so in a way that respects the personal boundaries of others. Assertive people are also willing to defend themselves against aggressive people.

Communication

Assertive communication involves respect for the boundaries of oneself and others. It also presumes an interest in the fulfilment of needs and wants through cooperation.

ASSERTIVE PEOPLE

Assertive people tend to have these characteristics.

- They feel free to express their feelings, thoughts and desires.

- They are able to initiate and maintain comfortable relationships.

- They know their rights.

- They have control over their anger.

- Assertive people are willing to compromise with others, rather than always wanting their own way.

- They tend to have good self-esteem.

- They enter friendships from an 'I count my needs…I count your needs…' position.

How To Be Assertive

Assertiveness is a skill that takes practice. It may always be easier for you to swallow your feelings, scream at someone or give them the silent treatment. But assertiveness is a better strategy. It works because it shows respect for oneself and others.

Through assertiveness, we develop contact with ourselves and with others. We become real human beings with real ideas, real differences and real flaws. And we admit all of these things. We don't try to become someone else's mirror. We don't try to suppress someone else's uniqueness. We don't try to pretend that we're perfect. We become ourselves.

11

Where To Begin?

Here are some ideas to get you started.

Start Small

Going unprepared just sets you up for failure. Try to be assertive in mildly tense situations, such as requesting to be seated at a different table at a restaurant. Then gently work up to tougher situations.

Learn To Say 'No'

People worry that saying 'No' is selfish. It's not. Rather, setting healthy limits is important to having healthy relationships.

Let Go Of Guilt

Being assertive can be tough—especially if you've been passive or a people pleaser most of your life. The first few times, it can be unnerving. But remember that being assertive is vital to your well-being. Assertive behaviour that involves advocating for oneself in a way that is respectful of others, is not wrong—it is healthy self-care.

Express Your Needs And Feelings

Don't assume that someone will automatically know what you need. You have to tell them. Be specific, clear, honest and respectful.

Check The Resources

Check out resources on assertiveness.

NEGATIVES

If your style is passive, you may seem to be shy or overly easy-going. You may routinely say things such as 'I'll just go with whatever the group decides.'

You tend to avoid conflict. Why is that a problem?

Because the message you're sending is that your thoughts and feelings aren't as important as those of other people. In essence, when you're too passive, you give others the license to disregard your wants and needs.

If your style is aggressive, you may come across as a bully who disregards the needs, feelings and opinions of others. You may appear self-righteous or superior. Aggressive people humiliate and intimidate others and may even be physically threatening. Aggression undercuts trust and mutual respect. Others may come to resent you, leading them to avoid or oppose you.

If you communicate in a passive-aggressive manner, you may say 'Yes' when you want to say 'No'. You may be sarcastic or complain about others behind their backs. Rather than confront an issue directly, you may show your anger and feelings through your actions or negative attitude. You may have developed a passive-aggressive style because you're uncomfortable being direct about your needs and feelings.

12

Benefits Of Being Assertive

Being assertive has many benefits.

Behaving assertively can help you:

- gain self-confidence and self-esteem.

- understand and recognise your feelings.

- earn respect from others.

- improve communication.

- create win-win situations.

- improve decision-making skills.

- create honest relationships.

- gain more job satisfaction.

Learning to be more assertive can also help you to effectively express your feelings when communicating with others.

LEARNING TO BE MORE ASSERTIVE

People develop different styles of communication based on their life experiences. Your style may be so ingrained that you may not even be aware of it. People tend to stick to the same communication style over time. But if you want to change your communication style, you can learn to communicate in healthier and more effective ways.

Assess Your Style

Do you voice your opinions or remain silent? Do you say 'Yes' to additional work even when your plate is full? Are you quick to judge or blame? Do people seem to dread or fear talking to you? Understand your style before you begin making changes.

Use 'I' Statements

Using 'I' statements lets others know what you're thinking without sounding accusatory. For instance, say, 'I disagree,' rather than, 'You're wrong.'

Practice Saying 'No'

If you have a hard time turning down requests, try saying 'No, I can't do that now.' Don't hesitate—be direct. If an explanation is appropriate, keep it brief.

Rehearse What You Want To Say

If it's challenging to say what you want or think, practise typical scenarios you encounter. Say what you want to say out loud. It may help to write it out first too, so you can practice from a script. Consider role-playing with a friend or colleague and ask for feedback.

Use Body Language

Communication isn't just verbal. Act confident even if you aren't feeling so. Keep an upright posture, but lean forward a bit. Make eye contact. Maintain a neutral or positive facial expression. Don't move your hands or use dramatic gestures. Practise assertive body language in front of a mirror or with a friend or colleague.

Keep Emotions In Check

Conflict is hard for most people. Maybe you get angry or frustrated, or maybe you feel like crying. Although these feelings are normal, they can get in the way of resolving conflict. If you feel too emotional going into a situation, wait a bit if possible. Then, work on remaining calm. Breathe slowly. Keep your voice even and firm.

When You Need Help Being Assertive

Remember, learning to be assertive takes time and practice. If you've spent years silencing yourself, becoming more assertive, probably, won't happen overnight. Or if anger leads you to be too aggressive, you may need to learn some anger-management techniques.

If despite your best efforts, you're not making progress towards becoming more assertive, consider formal assertiveness training.

13

Modes Of Communication

Basically, there are three modes of communication we can use. However, most of us probably predominantly behave and communicate in one of these modes.

SUBMISSIVE MODE

Submissive mode is a way of communicating that demonstrates lack of respect for one's own needs and rights. Most submissive people do not express their needs, or do so in such an apologetic and diffident manner that they are often ignored and not taken seriously. Sometimes a submissive person will think that they have communicated clearly when in reality their message was so vague and unclear that it was not understood at all. The pay-off for submissive communication is that the person gets to avoid conflict. For some people, submission is a way of avoiding, delaying or hiding the kind of conflict that is very scary to some people. Most people have been trained for submission by parents, older siblings, teachers and others. Submissive people are often praised; they are called 'nice', 'unselfish' and 'good sports'. It is important to note that submissive people often 'win' and control others through their seeming niceness and weakness. They get to have what they want by having the least amount of responsibility and avoiding conflict at the same time. There is also a price for being 'nice'. Submissive people go along with everyone's wishes and needs. Their relationships tend to not be as intimate and satisfying as those of others; a relationship requires two people and the submissive person is almost not there. People may like and praise the submissive person who voices no complaints for a while, but eventually the other person may start to feel guilty about being selfish or taking advantage of the submissive person. This feeling can then turn into pity, irritation and anger. Submissive people themselves, lose affection for others, eventually, because they feel a lack of fulfilment.

AGGRESSIVE MODE

Aggressive mode is an expression of feelings, needs and ideas in a way that goes against the other person. It is a 'move against' people or a 'move with the intent to hurt'.

Aggressive people try to get their needs met, even at the expense of others' needs. Aggressive communication and behaviour pay off in three major ways.

- Aggressive people tend to get their material needs met.
- They are able to protect their space.
- They seem to have control over their lives and the lives of others.

There are also several downsides to aggression.

- Aggressive people are very fearful.
- People are aggressive not because they feel strong, but because they feel weak.

- They tend to make enemies.

- Their aggression ultimately makes them even more vulnerable and fearful.

- Aggressive people tend to alienate people and are usually not liked or loved.

This alienation is a very powerful reason to deal with this issue. Too much aggression can also have serious consequences on one's health and creates an unsafe world for all to live in.

ASSERTIVE MODE

Assertive mode is a method of communication which enables a person to maintain self-respect, clearly communicate and pursue their needs, and defend their rights and personal space without abusing or dominating others. It confirms one's right to put forward one's needs, desires, ideas and feelings.

Assertiveness has a number of benefits. Assertive people usually like themselves more than the other two types. There is a connection between the ability to assert yourself and improved self-esteem. Assertiveness usually fosters better relationships by making a person more comfortable with themselves and, therefore, more comfortable to be around. Assertiveness greatly reduces fear and anxiety, and enables people to send positive energy towards each other.

The greatest benefit of assertiveness is the feeling of living one's own life. Your chances of getting what you want out of life improve greatly if you can let others know what you want and need, as well as how you feel.

Learning assertiveness takes effort and can be a struggle. It is not easy to change our way of communication. It can also be very painful to communicate vulnerably and honestly what you need, want or feel, and have that lead to conflict or rejection. In order to be assertive, you must be willing to risk enduring a conflict in order to forge a more authentic, intimate and dependable connection.

The choice to work on becoming more assertive is not an easy one. But it is the only possible way to take charge of one's life and break out of a rut of compulsive behaviours learnt in dysfunctional relationships. Assertion helps people to develop the power of having and making a choice, as well as learning to respect that choice in others. Assertiveness is better most of the time.

ADVANTAGES OF ASSERTIVE COMMUNICATION

- It helps us feel good about ourselves and others.
- It leads to development of mutual respect with others.
- It increases our self-esteem.
- It helps us achieve our goals.
- It minimises hurting and alienating other people.
- It reduces anxiety.
- It protects us from being taken advantage of by others.
- It enables us to make decisions and free choices in life.
- It enables us to express, both verbally and non-verbally, a wide range of feelings and thoughts, both positive and negative.

DISADVANTAGES
OF ASSERTIVE COMMUNICATION

Others may not approve of this style of communication or may not approve of the views you express.

Also, having a healthy regard for another person's rights means that you won't always get what you want.

You may also find out that you were wrong about a view point that you held.

There are six main characteristics of assertive communication.

- Eye contact: demonstrates interest; shows sincerity

- Body posture: congruent body language reinforces the significance of the message

- Gestures: appropriate gestures help to add emphasis

- Voice: a level, well-modulated tone is more convincing and acceptable, and is not intimidating

- Timing: use your judgement to maximise receptivity and impact

- Content: how, where and when you choose to comment is probably more important than what you say

THE PERFECT PARADIGM

Because assertiveness is based on mutual respect, it's an effective and diplomatic communication style. Being assertive shows that you respect yourself because you're willing to stand up for your interests and express your thoughts and feelings.

Importance of assertiveness in an organisation

Assertiveness	Stakeholders
• Personal identity	• Self
• Wages or salary	• Managers
• Satisfaction from exercising skills	• Colleagues
• Satisfaction from helping people	• Subordinates
• Social environment	• Clients or customers

14

Being Assertive

Assertiveness is the antidote to fear. It is the antidote to shyness and passivity. Assertiveness is to speak up, make requests, ask for favours and generally insist that your rights be respected as a significant, equal human being. It is fears and self-deprecation that keeps you from doing these things.

Assertiveness is the spirit to ask 'why' and question authority or tradition. However, this is not an attempt to rebel; it is a means to assume responsibility for asserting your share of control of the situation and to make things better.

HOW DO WE BUILD ASSERTIVENESS?

There are ways to become more assertive in your everyday interactions with others.

- Realise where changes are needed and believe in your rights.

- Try to figure out appropriate ways of asserting yourself in each situation that concerns you.

- Practise giving assertive responses.

All of us should insist on being treated fairly; we have to stand up for our rights without violating the rights of others.

This means tactfully, justly and effectively expressing our preferences, needs, opinions and feelings. This is called being 'assertive,' as distinguished from being unassertive (weak, passive, compliant and self-sacrificing) or aggressive (self-centred, inconsiderate, hostile and arrogantly demanding).

PURPOSE

Assertiveness is a positive aspect and has its own paradigms.

- To express negative emotions and to refuse requests
- To show positive emotions (joy, pride, liking and attraction) and to pay and accept compliments
- To initiate, carry on, change and terminate conversations comfortably
- To deal with minor irritations before your anger builds up intense resentment and explosive aggression

Assertiveness is a healthy way of communicating. It's the ability to speak up for ourselves in a way that is honest and respectful. Every day, we're in situations where being assertive can help us, such as approaching a teacher with a question or doing well in a job or college interview.

Being assertive doesn't come naturally to everyone. Some people communicate in a way that is too passive. Others have a style that is too aggressive. An assertive style is the happy medium between these two.

An assertive communication style can help us do the things we want to do. But it goes further than that... By being assertive, we show that we respect ourselves and other people.

Here's what it means to be assertive:

- You can give an opinion or say how you feel.

- You can ask for what you want or need.

- You can disagree respectfully.

- You can offer your ideas and suggestions.

- You can say 'No' without feeling guilty.

- You can speak up for someone else.

Remember:

- People who speak assertively send the message that they believe in themselves. They're not too timid and they're not too pushy. They know that their feelings and ideas matter. They're confident.

- People who are assertive tend to make friends more easily. They communicate in a way that respects other people's needs as well as their own. They tend to be better at working out conflicts and disagreements.

- People who give respect, get respect in return.

TOO PASSIVE? TOO AGGRESSIVE? OR JUST RIGHT?

How do you know where you fall on the assertiveness scale? Here are some examples.

Nikita has a style that's too passive. If you ask Nikita what movie she wants to see, she's most likely to say, 'I don't know…which one do you want to watch?' She usually lets others decide things, but later she regrets not saying what she wanted. It bothers her that her friends do most of the talking. But when Nikita tries to break into the conversation, she speaks so softly that others talk over her without realising.

Ruby has a style that's too aggressive. She has no trouble speaking her mind. But when she does, she comes across as loud and opinionated. Ruby dominates the conversation, often interrupts and rarely listens. If she disagrees with you, she lets you know—usually with sarcasm or a put-down. She has a reputation for being bossy and insensitive.

Richard has an assertive style. When you ask for his opinion, he gives it honestly. If he disagrees with you, he'll say so, but in a way that doesn't put you down. Richard is interested in your opinion, too. He listens to what you have to say. Even when he disagrees with you, you still feel he respects your point of view.

PROBLEMS OF BEING TOO PASSIVE

People who act too passively often end up feeling taken advantage of. They may begin to feel hurt, angry or resentful.

When you hold back what you think and feel, others don't get to know or understand you as well as they could. The group doesn't benefit from your inputs or ideas.

If you start to feel like your opinions or feelings don't count, it can lower your confidence and rob you of the chance to get recognition and positive feedback for your good ideas.

This can even lead to feeling depressed.

Here are a few things that can influence people to act too passively.

- A lack of confidence in themselves or the value of their opinions

- Worrying too much about pleasing others or being liked

- Worrying whether others will disagree with or reject their ideas and opinions

- Feeling sensitive to criticism or hurt by past experiences when their ideas were ignored or rejected

PROBLEMS OF BEING TOO AGGRESSIVE

People who come across as too aggressive can find it difficult to keep friends. They may dominate conversations or give their opinions too boldly and forcefully, leaving others feeling put off or disrespected. People with an aggressive style may get other people to do things their way, but many times they end up being rejected or disliked. They often lose the respect of others.

Here are a few things that can influence people to act too aggressively.

- Being overconfident

- Focusing too much on getting their needs met and their opinions across

- Not respecting or considering other people's views or needs

- Not knowing how to ask for input from others

WHY ISN'T EVERYONE ASSERTIVE?

Why do some people have assertive communication styles while others are more passive or aggressive? Part of it's just personality. The habits we develop or the experiences we have are another part. But we also learn to be assertive, passive or aggressive by watching how others act—especially our peers.

Here are a few things that can lead people to act assertively.

- Self-confidence
- Believing that their opinions count, their ideas and feelings matter, and they have the right to express themselves
- Being resilient (able to deal with criticism, rejection and setbacks)
- Respecting the preferences and needs of others
- Having role models for assertiveness
- Knowing their ideas were welcomed or assertiveness rewarded in the past

BEING MORE ASSERTIVE

Being assertive is a matter of practising certain communication skills and having the right attitude.

Some people are naturally more skilful when it comes to being assertive. Others need more practice. But everyone can improve.

How To Improve?

Start by considering which communication style (assertive, passive or aggressive) comes closest to yours. Then decide whether you need to work on being less passive, less aggressive, or simply need to build on your naturally assertive style.

To work on being less passive and more assertive:

- pay attention to what you think, feel, want and prefer. You need to be aware of these things before you can communicate them to others.

- notice if you say 'I don't know', 'I don't care' or 'It doesn't matter' when someone asks what you want. Practice saying what you'd prefer, especially on things that hardly matter. For example, if someone asks, 'Would you like green or red?' you can say, 'I'd prefer the green one; thanks.'

- practise asking for things. For example: 'Can you please pass me a spoon?', 'I need a pen; does anyone have an extra?' and 'Can you save me a seat?' This builds your skills and confidence for when you need to ask for something more important.

- Give your opinion. Say whether or not you liked a movie you saw and why.

- Practice using 'I' statements, such as 'I'd like...', 'I prefer...' or 'I feel...'

Remind yourself that your ideas and opinions are as important as everyone else's. Knowing this, helps you be assertive.

Assertiveness starts with an inner attitude of valuing yourself as much as you value others.

To work on being less aggressive and more assertive:

- try letting others speak first.

- notice if you interrupt. Catch yourself and say: 'Oh, sorry; go ahead!' and let the other person finish.

- ask someone else's opinion, then listen to the answer.

- when you disagree, try to say so without putting down the other person's point of view. For example, instead of saying: 'That's a stupid idea,' try 'I don't really like that idea.' Or instead of saying: 'He's such a jerk,' try 'I think he's insensitive.'

- notice when you're best at being assertive. People behave differently in different situations. In tougher situations, try thinking, 'What would I say to my close friends?'

When you speak assertively, it shows you believe in yourself. Building assertiveness is one step to becoming your best self, the person you want to be! Even naturally assertive people can build and expand their skills.

15

Draw The Fine Line

'Work with people, not against them.' This is the key mantra to assertiveness.

Do you consider yourself to be assertive? What does being assertive mean to you? Does it mean exercising your rights all the time, every time? Or does it mean knowing when to let someone else or some other cause/outcome take precedence over your rights?

It's not always easy to identify truly assertive behaviour. This is because there is a fine line between assertiveness and aggression.

Assertiveness is based on balance: It requires being forthright about your wants and needs while still considering the rights, needs and wants of others. When you are assertive, you ask for what you want but you don't necessarily get it.

Aggressive behaviour is based on winning: It requires that you do what is in your own best interest without regard for the rights, needs, feelings or desires of others. When you are aggressive, you take what you want regardless and you don't usually ask.

Assertiveness is a skill that can be learned: Developing your assertiveness starts with a good understanding of who you are and a belief in the value you bring. When you have that, you have the basis of self-confidence. Assertiveness helps to build on that self-confidence and improves your relationships at work.

Assertive people:

- get to 'win-win' more easily. They see the value in their opponent and his/her position, and can quickly find a common ground.

- are better problem-solvers. They feel empowered to do whatever it takes to find the best solution.

- are less stressed. They know they have personal power and they don't feel threatened or victimised when things don't go as planned or expected.

- are doers. They get things done because they know they can.

When you act assertively, you act fairly and with empathy. The power you use comes from your self-assurance and not from intimidation or bullying. When you treat others with fairness and respect, you get the same treatment in return. You are well liked and people see you as a leader and someone they want to work with.

DEVELOPING ASSERTIVENESS

Some people are naturally more assertive than others.

If your disposition tends more towards being either passive or aggressive, you need to work on these skills.

- Value yourself and your rights.

- Understand that your rights, thoughts, feelings, needs and desires are just as important as everyone else's. But remember that they are not more important than anyone else's, either.

- Recognise your rights and protect them.

- Believe that you deserve to be treated with respect and dignity at all times.

- Stop apologising for everything.

- Identify your needs and wants, and ask for them to be satisfied.

- Don't wait for someone to recognise what you need. (You might have to wait forever!)

- Understand that to perform to your full potential, your needs must be met.

- Find ways to get your needs met without sacrificing others' needs in the process.

- Acknowledge that people are responsible for their own behaviour.

- Don't make the mistake of accepting responsibility for how people react to your assertive statements (with anger and resentment). You can only control yourself.

- As long as you are not violating someone else's needs, you have the right to say or do what you want.

- Express negative thoughts and feelings in a healthy and positive manner.

- Allow yourself to be angry, but always be respectful.

- Do say what's on your mind, but do it in a way that does not hurt the other person.

- Control your emotions.

- Stand up for yourself and confront people, who challenge you and/or your rights.

- Receive criticism and compliments positively.

- Accept compliments graciously.

- Allow yourself to make mistakes and ask for help.

- Accept feedback positively. Be prepared to say you don't agree but do not get defensive or angry.

- Learn to say 'No' when you need to.

- Know your limits and what will cause you to feel taken advantage of.

- Know that you can't do everything or please everyone and learn to be okay with that.

- Go with what is right for you.

- Suggest an alternative for a 'win-win' solution.

ASSERTIVE COMMUNICATION TECHNIQUES

There are a variety of ways to communicate assertively. These can easily be adapted to any situation you are facing.

'I' Statements

Use 'I want...', 'I need...' or 'I feel...' to convey basic assertions.

For example: I feel strongly that we need to bring in a third party to mediate this disagreement.

Empathy

First, recognise how the other person views the situation, then express what you need.

I understand that you are having trouble working with Andy, however, this project needs to be completed by Friday. Let's all sit down and come up with a plan to get it done.

Escalation

This type of assertiveness is necessary when your first attempts are not successful in getting your needs met.

The technique involves getting more and more firm with time. It may end in you telling the other person what you will do next, if you are not satisfied. Remember though, you may not get what you want in the end.

Rohit, this is the third time this week I've had to speak to you about arriving late. If you are late one more time this month, I will activate the disciplinary process.

Ask For More Time

Sometimes, you just need to put off saying anything. You might be too emotional or you might really not know what you want. Be honest and tell the person you need a few minutes to compose your thoughts.

Ajit, your request has caught me off guard. I'll get back to you within half an hour.

Change Your Verbs

Use 'won't' instead of 'can't'.

Use 'want' instead of 'need'.

Use 'choose to' instead of 'have to'.

Use 'could' instead of 'should'.

Broken Record

Prepare ahead of time the message you want to convey, for instance, 'I cannot take on any more projects right now.'

During the conversation, keep restating your message using the same language over and over again. Don't relent. Eventually, the person is likely to realise that you really mean what you are saying.

- I would like you to work on the Clancy project.
- I'll pay extra for you accommodating me.
- Seriously, this is really important, my boss insists it gets done.
- Will you do it as a personal favour?
- I'm sorry, I value our past relationship but I simply cannot take on any more projects right now.

Remember: Be careful with the broken record technique. If you use it to protect yourself from exploitation, that's good. However, if you use it to bully someone into taking action that's against their interest—it's manipulative and dishonest.

Scripting

This technique involves preparing your responses using a four-pronged approach.

- **Event:** Tell the other person exactly how you see a situation or problem.

- **Feelings:** Describe how you feel and express your emotions clearly.

- **Needs:** Tell the other person what you need so they don't have to guess.

- **Consequences:** Describe the positive outcome if your needs are fulfilled.

Once you are clear about what you want to say and express, it is much easier to actually do it.

Key points

Being assertive means knowing where the fine line is between assertion and aggression and balancing on it. It means having a strong understanding of yourself and acknowledging that you deserve to get what you want. And it means standing up for yourself even in the most difficult situations.

As your assertiveness improves, so will your productivity and efficiency. Start today and begin to see how being assertive allows you to work with people to accomplish tasks, solve problems and reach solutions.

PERFECT APPRAISAL

Performance appraisal is the process of evaluating and documenting one's performance on the job. It is part of career development. This book deals with the appraisal process, training for appraisal, pitfalls in appraisal and the dos and don'ts of appraisal.

Perfect Appraisal provides simple techniques to a perfect appraisal with a holistic approach.

PERFECT COMMUNICATION

Communication is the process of sharing information, knowledge or meaning. What matters most is the 'response-ability'; response is more important than the message. Listeners must not just hear; they must listen. This book deals with speaking skills, writing skills and listening skills.

Perfect Communication is much more than just this.

PERFECT CV

A curriculum vitae (CV) or résumé presents a record of your qualities, skills and experience to an employer, so that your suitability for a particular job can be assessed. In Latin, 'curriculum vitae' means 'the way your life has run' and 'résumé' is the French word for 'summary'. This book deals with making a CV special, writing a CV with lack of experience, tailoring a CV and digital and online CVs.

Perfect CV helps you to compile your CV and suggests ways to improve it.

PERFECT LEADER

If you want to inspire, motivate and engage, and move people into action, leadership is the ability you require. Leaders set direction and develop the skill to guide people to the right destination. This book spells out leadership styles, initiatives that are needed, proactive tools, the importance of perseverance and methods to step out of the comfort zone.

Perfect Leader helps you to inspire the vision of the future as a leader. It equips you to make strategic decisions, shape conflict and find your competitive edge.

PERFECT MEETING

Meetings help one to build rapport. They are a forum for inter-learning and understanding; a platform to share information. *Perfect Meeting* is about the basic skills of management. This book deals with effective meetings, conference meetings, stand-up meetings, one-on-one meetings and the tasks and skills of the chairperson.

Perfect Meeting helps you generate cooperation and commitment to attain higher levels of performance.

PERFECT NEGOTIATION

In order to settle differences, one needs to master the skill of negotiation. Without this skill, conflicts and disagreements will arise. This book deals with the process of negotiation and its different stages: preparation, discussion, goals, win-win outcome and agreement.

Perfect Negotiation helps you master the different types of negotiation formats, styles, and preparing strategies for negotiation.

PERFECT PRESENTATION

Presentation skills are critical as they help one to inform, motivate and inspire others. It is a means to get a message across to the listeners, with a persuasive element. This book talks about the canons of persuasive presentations, verbal and non-verbal communication, styles of presentation and the opening and closing of a presentation.

Perfect Presentation helps you master the art of making effective presentations.